YOUR KNOWLEDGE HAS VALUE

- We will publish your bachelor's and master's thesis, essays and papers

- Your own eBook and book - sold worldwide in all relevant shops

- Earn money with each sale

Upload your text at www.GRIN.com and publish for free

Bibliographic information published by the German National Library:

The German National Library lists this publication in the National Bibliography; detailed bibliographic data are available on the Internet at http://dnb.dnb.de .

This book is copyright material and must not be copied, reproduced, transferred, distributed, leased, licensed or publicly performed or used in any way except as specifically permitted in writing by the publishers, as allowed under the terms and conditions under which it was purchased or as strictly permitted by applicable copyright law. Any unauthorized distribution or use of this text may be a direct infringement of the author s and publisher s rights and those responsible may be liable in law accordingly.

Imprint:

Copyright © 2018 GRIN Verlag
Print and binding: Books on Demand GmbH, Norderstedt Germany
ISBN: 9783668628267

This book at GRIN:

https://www.grin.com/document/388632

Hang Le

Gap Between Mental and Physical Health

GRIN Verlag

GRIN - Your knowledge has value

Since its foundation in 1998, GRIN has specialized in publishing academic texts by students, college teachers and other academics as e-book and printed book. The website www.grin.com is an ideal platform for presenting term papers, final papers, scientific essays, dissertations and specialist books.

Visit us on the internet:

http://www.grin.com/

http://www.facebook.com/grincom

http://www.twitter.com/grin_com

Gap between Mental Health and Physical Health

Hang Le

Saint Francis University

April 29, 2017

Gap between Mental Health and Physical Health

Introduction

Within health care, mental illnesses have not been readily accepted as an exclusive field of medicine. Even more so, there are still many speculations about the need to care for or maintain the state of one's mental or emotional well-being when compared to the importance of seeking immediate treatment for physical indications. Such divergence in viewpoints requires a more thorough understanding of the biological and psychological aspects, not as separate components, but rather as interdependent. According to Vaughn, mental or emotional health refers to an individual's overall psychological well-being, which includes the way they feel about themselves, the quality of their relationships, and their ability to manage feelings and handle hardships (2014). As for physical health, it can be viewed as the state of an individual's body to function without limitations or complaints.

Although mental health concentrates on the emotional and behavioral conditions and physical health focuses on the biological causative factors, they share commonality in the sense that issues with mental health can present with many different symptoms, just like issues with physical health; there are mental status exams like there are physical examinations. There are tests that can be done to assess mental health and the same as with physical health (Vaughn, 2014). The main determining factor as to why mental health and illness are often overlooked and disregarded lies in the reality that most people visit a doctor for physical problems and monthly check-ups, but majority of them do not regularly turn to mental health professionals for care until after a crisis has happened. Thus, it is crucial to identify and analyze the underlying reasons for such inconsistency. The lack of recognition for mental illnesses and awareness of one's mental and emotional health have various contributing factors. There are societal views and ethical concerns that surround the possible causes for the inequality of care and attention given to the psychological health approaches.

Literature Review

Due to the fact that many may view mental health as a rare phenomenon because most of the illnesses encompassing the mind, emotions, and behaviors have not been given the proper acknowledgement as it deserves in modern medicine, it is necessary to trace the origin of mental illness. The early history of mental illnesses dates as far back in time to when ancient Egyptian, Indian, Greek, and Romans writings and cultures categorized mental illness as a well-known supernatural phenomena resulting from demonic possession by the evil spirits or a form of religious punishment (Stanley, 2015). The most commonly believed manner for healing from the illnesses was rooted in religious superstitions. Many practiced precautionary measures like upholding personal hygiene and preserving "purity of the mind and body in order to prevent and protect one from diseases" (2015). Nonetheless, these influential and practical actions were soon put to rest when the Greeks transformed the way that psychological disorders were perceived by its methodology of treatment. When the philosopher and physician, Hippocrates, studied mental illness and discovered in the 5th century B.C. that illnesses come from natural occurrences in the body, he then shifted away from the superstitious beliefs and moved towards the medical aspect of the pathology of the brain and the imbalances in the body that suggestively contribute to varying conditions of mental illness (2015). Hippocrates eventually led the way in treating mentally ill individuals with the focus to alter their surroundings or administer certain substances as medications. Nevertheless, there remained a large proportion of people who still believed in the supernatural causes and utilized alternative treatments despite Hippocrates' ground breaking findings.

As history moved along, the establishment of mental health hospitals helped to reduce barriers to treatment and care services. Around the 1840s, after witnessing the dangerous and unhealthy conditions in which many mentally ill patients lived, activist Dorothea Dix successfully persuaded the U.S. government to fund the building of 32 state psychiatric hospitals (Unite for Sight, 2015). These state hospitals became an effective care model as it was a considerably useful gateway for patient access to mental health services. Shortly thereafter, more efforts and initiatives were accounted for in working to improve the U.S. mental health care system and policy. In 1909, the founder of Mental Health America (MHA), Clifford Beers, worked to improve the lives of the mentally ill in the United States through research and lobbying efforts (2015). Then in 1946, Harry Truman made his contribution by passing the National Mental Health Act, which created the National Institute of Mental Health and allocating government funds toward research (2015). With the dedication of these early historical roles along with many other reformists after them, it set into action a movement that shaped the transformation of mental health. Yet, much of what is known today regarding mental illnesses has not allow for it to gain popularity among most cultures solely because conversations about mental ailments and patients are subjects to be avoided or cast aside.

Since mental illness is perceived through social perspectives as a disease of the mind, it is only plausible to survey the brain pathology in an attempt to justify the inaccuracy of society's ways of thinking about mental health. And while it is logical to inspect the mind as being the culprit of mental illness, it is nearly impractical to not challenge the relation that exists between the mind and body. The concept of mind-body connection asserts that the mind and body is not a one-way road, but rather it is a two-way street. In accordance with Sartini-Cprek, "researchers began revisiting the mind-body connection in the late 20th century, and since then, they have compiled an impressive amount of data that indicates our bodies and minds share a common chemical language and are constantly communicating with each other" (2017). Further in her article, Sartini-Cprek also provides three approaches in which research demonstrates the connection between the mind and body. These examples include the effect of chronic stress, the placebo effect, and the gut health.

    Chronic stress is the first and foremost obvious example. Stress, whether it would be mentally or emotionally, is often times a necessary reaction when faced with the responsibilities of daily life. And for the most part, our bodies are designed to cope with stress on a minimal level. On the other hand, when the level of stress reaches a state of chronicity, then at this point the body is not well-equipped to response and begins to experience certain consequences like an increase in heart rate, rapid breathing, muscle tension, elevated blood pressure, headaches, stomach aches, sleep problems, chest pain, fatigue, changes in sex drive, and a rise in cortisol hormones, which researchers have associated it with serious health issues (Sartini-Cprek, 2017). The placebo effect is another common example. This is a phenomenon of an experimental approach that yields a beneficial effect of improved symptoms after taking a medication that contains no ingredients. Dr. Lissa Rankin, founder of the Whole Health Medicine Institute and author of *Mind Over Medicine: Scientific Proof That You Can Heal Yourself*, "reported patients in clinical trials who received sugar pills, saline injections or fake surgeries, but believe they might be getting the new wonder drug or miracle surgery, get better 18% to 80% of the time" (2017). Another way of how the mind can affect the body's ability to function properly is demonstrated in the gut. The study of gut health is an up-and-coming field within medicine where researchers and doctors are finding new connections with the gastrointestinal tract and mental health. As Sartini-Cprek mentions, the gut is often considered as the "second brain" due to the fact that there is a network of 100 million neurons that line the gut. And as a result, it produces 95% of the serotonin and 50% of the dopamine in the body (2017). Sartini-Cprek goes on to explain that these chemicals have been linked to the body's well-being and stress management. Therefore, a disruption or imbalance of these chemicals and the gastrointestinal microbiota may lead to depression, but a positive effect on mental health may result when there is a balance of gut bacteria to enhance nutrient absorption (2017). From understanding the relationship behind the mind and body, it paints a clearer illustration of how mental health and physical health are alike and should be treated equally in the domain of medicine.

    Following the discussion on the mind-body connection, there are a variety of conditions and pathologies that also exemplify the correlation between biological diseases and psychological disorders. One prime illustration of a mental health condition is depression. As stated by Collingwood, depression and other physical health conditions have separate but additive effects on well-being since patients with both problems are at particular risk because the physical issue can complicate depression's assessment and treatment by masking or mimicking its symptoms (2016). Furthermore, several studies are done to provide statistical data interlinking mental illness and physical problem. There is a 2009 study of patients with severe chronic obstructive pulmonary disease (COPD) found that 22% of the participants had at least mild depression of a score of 14 or more based on the Beck Depression Inventory and among these, 17% were taking anti-depressants (2016). In another 2003 study, it concludes that "the treatment of depression in arthritis patients led to improved arthritis-related pain intensity, less interference with daily activities and better overall health status and quality of life" (2016). These two studies show that patients with a biological diagnosis of physical symptoms are likely to present with some disturbance in their psychological state; and the same holds true when these features are reversed like when patients are being treated for a psychological disorder, their symptoms from a chronic physical disease tend to be alleviated. The important take-away from these examples is that a person's physical health can significantly affect their mental health, and vice versa.

     Moreover, mental health and physical health should not be thought of as separate because poor physical health increases the risk of mental health problems and similar consequences result when reversed. It has been observed that one of the clearest places that the association between mental and physical health is proven is in longevity (Bradley University, 2016). The effect of mental health on longevity is reflective in the different ways poor mental health has revealed to be detrimental to physical well-being. For instance, the Mental Health Foundation asserts that depression has been linked to 67% increased risk of death from heart disease and 50% increased risk of death from cancer as well as schizophrenia is associated with double the risk of death from heart disease and three times the risk of death from respiratory disease (2017). Additionally, psoriasis is among one of the conditions that impacts individual physically and psychologically in a recurring pattern. Given that psoriasis is an auto-immune disorder and commonly triggered by stress, approximately one third of the affected population experience anxiety and depression because the condition can cause emotional distress, which can trigger a psoriasis flare that can eventually result in further distress (Mental Health Foundation, 2017).

     The biological pathologies of physical conditions are widely acknowledged as illnesses that require medical treatment. Similarly, the exact stance should be valid when it comes to establishing mental health within our society, but the justification to seek care or treatment from a mental health professional is frequently overlooked because of the negative perceptions shared by the general public.

Apparently, mental health is more often than not viewed and regarded very differently than physical health. It is as though there is a distinction between a disorder and a feeling. This gap is created as a consequence of various barriers within the mental health. Such includes social stigma, discrimination in health coverage and services, and the moral concern of one's liberty. According to Unite for Sight, mental illness stigma is defined as the "devaluing, disgracing, and disfavoring by the general public of individuals with mental illnesses" (2015). In an effort to better understand the serious stigma that is attached to mental illness, it is critical to evaluate the sources that influentially affect how society disapproves of mental illness. Statistically speaking based on a claim by the Centers for Disease Control and Prevention (CDC), there are only one in four people with mental health issues who feel that other people are compassionate and sympathetic toward them (Holmes, 2016). The greater attribute of where the stigma stems from lies in the fact that there is a lack of understanding of mental disorder as physical illnesses. As many experts would agree that "part of the problem when it comes to criticizing someone's mental health is a lack of empathy and knowledge about the ailments" (2016). Another aspect that possibly contributes to such stigmatization is from cultural perspective.

For the most part, cultural perspectives and religious teachings quite often shape society's attitudes and influence one's beliefs about many different matters. In highlighting the cultural values pertaining to mental health across communities, the notion of favoritism cannot be dismissed. In an exceptional TedTalks presentation that is discussed by Guy Winch, a psychologist and author, he offers remarkable insight on the benefits of dealing with psychological pains and developing emotional resilience (Cord, 2016). With his presentation, he mentions the idea of favoritism as a concept that is seen everywhere in society. Nonetheless, the kind of favoritism that Winch refers to is one that focuses on how society values the body over the mind. In an example, Winch shares a story of a little 5-year-old boy he observed while staying overnight at a friend's home. As Winch watched his friend's son standing on a stool to brush his teeth, the little boy slipped and scratched his leg. Immediately after getting up from the fall, the little boy was seen reaching for a band-aid to put on his cut (TEDxLinnaeusUniversity, 2014). This story holds a profound meaning as it serves to illustrate how much emphasis and training have been instilled in all of us at such a young age to care for the well-being of our physical body; yet so little is taught to us about maintaining psychological health and emotional hygiene. Another instance can be depicted in a setting where if a person is depressed, society says "just shake it off; it's all in your head." But what if a person broke their leg, do we say "just walk it off, it's all in your leg?" (TEDxLinnaeusUniversity, 2014). This goes to demonstrate that we sustain both physical and psychological injuries, but it does not occur to us that we need to treat and address these psychological injuries with equal care and attention as we do with our physical injuries. And this is all simply because society places little value on teaching psychological self-care as a part of cultural upbringings.

Alongside the mental illness stigma, another form of discrimination takes ground in the unfair treatment and the disadvantages that result from being denied of resources. Due to the complex nature of psychological disorders, mental health care services are often not readily available or are under-utilized because of insufficient mental health care policies as well as limited availability of health professionals and limited affordability of mental health services (Unite for Sight, 2015). Given that in reference to payments by insurers, mental illnesses are often times being viewed as behavioral repertoires in which it creates for a discrepancy in health coverage for mental health. In accordance with Schuster, since the passing of the 2008 Mental Health Parity Act and the Affordable Care Act, mental health is supposed to be afforded the same coverage as physical health. However, one-quarter of the health plans that are being sold on health insurance exchanges set up through the Affordable Care Act do not equal benefits for general and mental health care (2015).

In addition to policy limitations and allocation of health budget for mental health, the question of autonomy poses significant hindrance in the disparity of views on mental and physical health. The main concern when it comes to seeking care, treatment, or management of these mental illnesses is where does society draws the fine line between being empathetic or enabling these behavioral responses. According to the American Foundation for Suicide Prevention, 90% or more people who have died by suicide had a mental disorder at the time of their deaths since these disorders had not been recognized, diagnosed, or adequately treated (Schuster, 2015). In an analogy of a person going to the gym to be physically fit, the same idea applies when a person goes to therapy or in-patient facilities to maintain their mental fitness. Too often, society fails to perceive mental and physical well-being as being alike. Thus, it alters the attitude individuals may have about seeking help because of the guilt and shame that is associated with mental illness. Their sense of freedom and control over their mental health is diminished and minimized. So, they eventually cave in to the principle that they can handle it on their own; but in reality, they become crippled by their emotions and fears.

The common barriers that cause society to have these negative outlooks on psychological disorders are the preventative factors that expand the gap between mental health and physical health even further and over time leads to unequal outcomes. By drawing upon these limitations, there are strategies that can be taken into account in order to maximize the effort of raising awareness of mental health, advocating for the mentally ill population, and optimizing care services. A large segment for resolving the inequality comes from educating the public about mental disorders. Limited knowledge about mental illness can prevent individuals from recognizing mental illness and seeking treatment as well as poor understanding of mental illness also impairs families' abilities to provide adequate care and support (Unite for Sight, 2015). Of equal importance as raising awareness through education is the willpower to advocate for more human rights and less stigma; and designing policies that are comprehensive with sufficient planning and investment to provide consistency in mental health services (2015).

In referencing back to the concept of mind-body connection, some of the recommended approaches for bridging the gap on psychological and physical health include exercising, meditating, journaling, sustaining regular sleep, and maintaining nutritional balance diet. Studies have shown that exercising is viewed as a natural anti-depressant and helps to increase activity in the hippocampus (part of the brain that contribute to spacial memory) as well as in the frontal lobes, where endorphins are released in the body and certain neurotransmitters are increasingly produced (Rheeders, 2014). Besides engaging in activities that help to improve the mind-body connection, it is also necessary to seek professional assistance, such as counseling and support group.

Summary

Based on the World Health Organization's definition of mental health, it is characterized as a "state of well-being in which every individual realizes his or her own potential, can cope with the normal stresses of life, can work productively and fruitfully, and is able to make a contribution to her or his community" (Wick, 2015). To review, the importance of maintaining mental well-being is precisely of equal value as physical health. The two are inseparable. Despite the expected norm that society holds on the viewpoints surrounding mental health, it is evident through history that the mind and body are understood to be in relation and treated as a whole. While in recent years, there is an increased of awareness and research on mental and physical well-being, there still remain a significant gap between the two because of social stigmas, limited accessibility, inadequate policies, and cultural bias that impedes one's ability to be self-sufficient. The integration of knowledge from the past and present can transform the way psychological illnesses are perceived in health care. Although the change does not come easy, the future for recognizing mental disorders and physical illnesses as equal is progressing in the direction that would gain societal acceptance.

References

Bradley University. (2016). How mental health affects physical health. Retrieved from http://onlinedegrees.bradley.edu/resources/articles/how-mental-health-affects-physical-health/

Collingwood, J. (2016). The Relationship between Mental and Physical Health. Psych Central. Retrieved from https://psychcentral.com/lib/the-relationship-between-mental-and-physical-health/

Cord, R. (2016). Bridging the Gap: Physical and Mental Health. Pacific MFT Network. Retrieved from http://www.pacificmft.com/single-post/2016/10/14/Bridging-the-Gap-Physical-Mental-Health

Holmes, L. (2016). What If People Treated Physical Illness Like Mental Illness? The Huffington Post. Retrieved from http://www.huffingtonpost.com/2014/11/13/mental-illness-physical-i_n_6145156.html

Mental Health Foundation. (2017). Physical health and mental health. Retrieved from https://www.mentalhealth.org.uk/a-to-z/p/physical-health-and-mental-health

Rheeders, E. (2014). How Physical Health Affects Mental Health. FedHealth. Retrieved from http://www.fedhealth.co.za/healthy-living-tips/how-physical-health-affects-mental-health/

Sartini-Cprek, N. (2017). The Mind-Body Connection: How Mental and Physical Wellness are Linked. Good Therapy. Retrieved from http://www.goodtherapy.org/blog/mind-body-connection-how-mental-physical-wellness-are-linked-0412174

Schuster, S. (2015). 4 Reasons Mental Illness and Physical Illness are Actually Super Different. The Mighty Proud Media, Inc. Retrieved from https://themighty.com/2015/11/how-mental-illness-and-physical-illness-are-different/

Stanley, T. (2015). A Beautiful Mind: The history of the treatment of mental illness. History Cooperative. Retrieved from http://historycooperative.org/a-beautiful-mind-the-history-of-the-treatment-of-mental-illness/

TEDxLinnaeusUniversity. (2014, November). *Why we all need to practice emotional first aid* [Video file]. Retrieved from https://www.ted.com/talks/guy_winch_the_case_for_emotional_hygiene?utm_source=ted comshare&utm_medium=referral&utm_campaign=tedspread

Unite for Sight. (2015). Module 2: A Brief History of Mental Illness and the U.S. Mental Health Care System. Retrieved from http://www.uniteforsight.org/mental-health/module2

Unite for Sight. (2015). Module 6: Barriers to Mental Health Care. Retrieved from http://www.uniteforsight.org/mental-health/module6

Unite for Sight. (2015). Module 7: Cultural Perspective on Mental Health. Retrieved from http://www.uniteforsight.org/mental-health/module7

Vaughn, K. (2014). Physical Health vs. Mental Health: Is One More Important? BJC Health Care. Retrieved from https://www.bjceap.com/Blog/ArtMID/448/ArticleID/93/Physical-Health-vs-Mental-Health-Is-One-More-Important

Wick, R. (2015). Bridging the Gap between Behavioral and Primary Health Care for Low-Income Patients. Health Affairs. Retrieved from http://healthaffairs.org/blog/2015/05/16/bridging-the-gap-between-behavioral-and-primary-health-care-for-low-income-patients/

YOUR KNOWLEDGE HAS VALUE

- We will publish your bachelor's and master's thesis, essays and papers

- Your own eBook and book - sold worldwide in all relevant shops

- Earn money with each sale

Upload your text at www.GRIN.com
and publish for free